Dump him,
Marry the HORSE!

Dump him,
Marry the HORSE!

WHY A HORSE IS A BETTER MATCH THAN A MAN

WILLOW CREEK PRESS

Published by Willow Creek Press
P.O. Box 147, Minocqua, Wisconsin 54548

Photo Credits:
AnimalsAnimals: page 8 © Donald Specker; page 12 © Carol Geake; page 19 © Eastcott/Momatiuk; page 41 © Eastcott/Momatiuk; page 46 © Jerry Cooke; page 53 © Dominique Braud; page 57 © Donald Specker; page 58 © Scott Smith; page 81 © Jim Tuten; page 88 © Gerard Lacz
Ardea.com: page 6 © Chris Harvey; page 14 © Chris Harvey; page 16 © Ardea.com; page 17 © John Daniels; page 21 © John Cancalosi; page 22 © Jean-Paul Ferrero; page 29 © Jean-Paul Ferrero; page 37 © Chris Harvey; page 40 © James Marchington; page 47 © John Daniels; page 49 © Ardea.com; page 51 © Chris Knights; page 65 © Yanin Arthus-Bertrand; page 79 © Hans D. Dossenbach; page 89 © Chris Harvey
© Denver Bryan/DenverBryan.com: pages 31, 91
© Robert Dawson: pages 13, 94
© Ron Kimball/ronkimballstock.com: pages 2, 28, 32, 61, 78
© Nancy McCallum: pages 26, 39, 48, 59, 68, 74, 80, 82, 83
© Londie G. Padelsky: pages 18, 23, 35, 44, 45, 50, 55, 62, 69, 70, 71, 72, 73, 77, 96
© Dusty L. Perin: pages 5, 9, 33, 36, 52, 60, 76, 84, 85, 90, 92
© Christiane Slawik: pages 20, 67, 86, 87
© Lynn M. Stone: pages 42, 43, 64
© Sabine Stuewer/www.stuewer-tierfoto.de: pages 10, 11, 15, 25, 27, 30, 34, 38, 54, 56, 66, 75, 95

Text by Melissa Sovey
Design: Donnie Rubo
Printed in Canada

SURE, men are great...

But chances are that from the time you were a little girl, you've been MORE head-over-heels for HORSES. The little boys from your childhood could never capture your affections like the wonderful, exciting, exhilarating notion of spending time with a horse.

OKAY, now ask yourself... **A**ren't there occasions to this day where you'd rather be hitched to your HORSE than your MAN? Along with being your first love, there are countless reasons WHY A HORSE IS A BETTER MATCH THAN A MAN. Here are just a few...

For starters...

A horse never complains about the same old meal.

He enjoys healthful food
and will diet with you!

H<small>e's</small> easy to please...

and will be eating from
your hand in no time!

A horse is affectionate...

fun-loving...

and adventuresome.

While he
loves a good
scratch...

he can handle that himself as well.

He is a great listener,

and a smooth talker.

He is
charmingly
goofy...

and nonchalantly handsome!

He has a great backside...

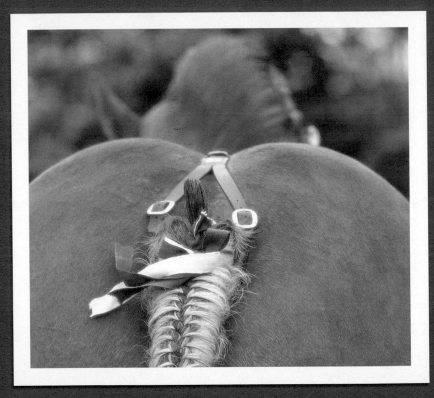

that will always be bigger than yours...

and he'll never make comments about your saddlebags because he has them too!

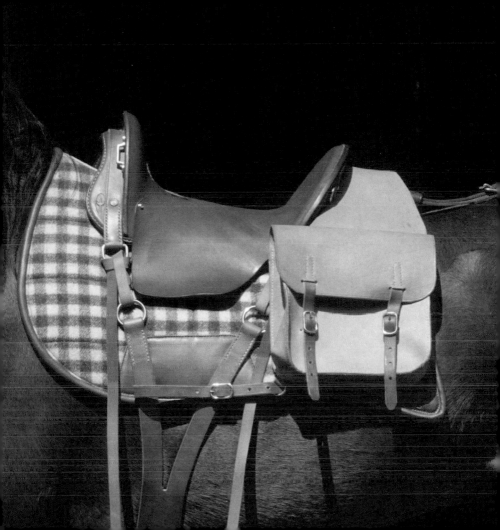

A horse comes when he's called...

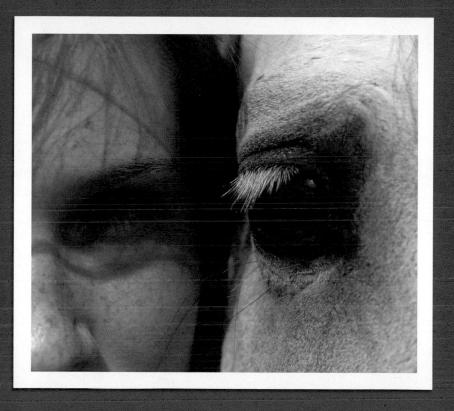

and only has eyes for you.

or at least match your stride.

He loves road trips...

and he understands "hit the trail"!

He'll wait patiently while you get ready to go out...

or hang out with you if
you want to stay home.

Being with a horse makes you feel
like you're on top of the world...

and closer to the earth.

A horse will expect you to take the reins...

and he will delight in your freedom!

Horses don't even mind if you are in love with more than one of them!

A horse will mow the grass with pleasure...

loves flowers and gardening...

pulls his weight with the chores...

and expects very little in return.

A horse will spend time
with you after work...

and he doesn't think "round-up"
means his next beer is waiting!

He has sweet friends that you don't mind if he brings home.

With a horse, size really doesn't matter...

and he has no performance anxiety!

While he looks pretty in pink,

he also looks like James Dean in leather!

Drooling is
a good sign...

and being unshaven is okay.

He smells great...

even better when he sweats!

He likes being clean...

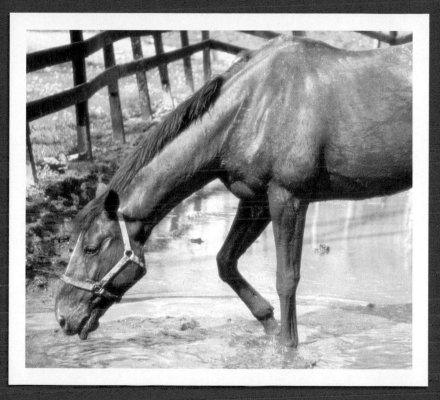

and, since he has his own place,
he doesn't track mud into the house.

is naturally romantic...

and always looks sexy!

OF COURSE,

horses are high maintenance...

They require a lot of space, tons of food, plenty of grooming, endless training, and constant attention. They can wail inconsolably when separated from their buddies and they can be very stubborn until they figure out that you are their leader...

But HOW is that different than a man?

A horse's "herd" is very important to him...

and posing for a family
portrait is not a chore!

He respects an alpha mare...

and appreciates when you take charge.

He mirrors your emotions...

and he is patient if you're
in one of your "moods."

He is great with kids...

he loves
your dog...

tolerates your cat...

and is always happy to meet your friends.

A horse doesn't mind girl talk...

and he can keep a secret.

A horse understands a little vanity...

and he's fun
to accessorize!

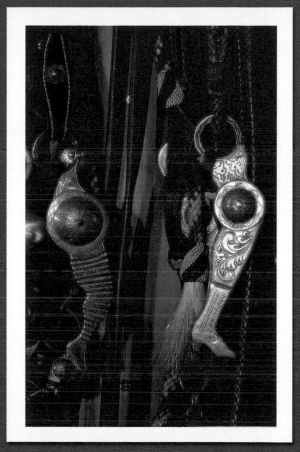

He understands the
delight of a salt scrub...

a new hair-do...

new shoes...

and fun
hats.

He also appreciates a good pedicure...

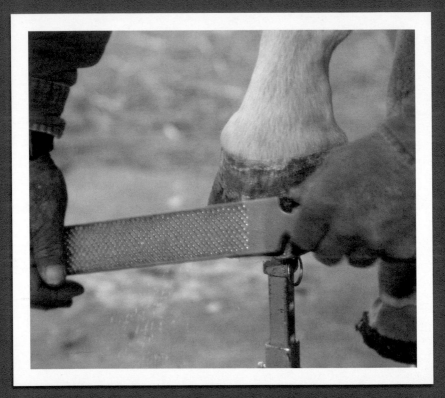

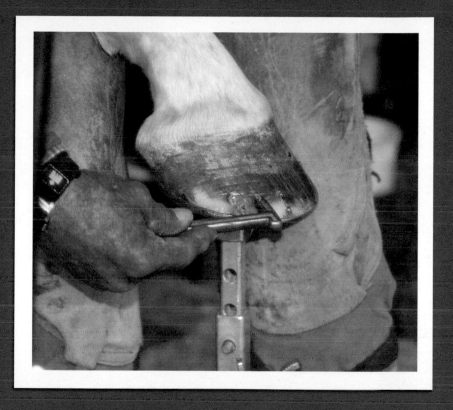

and taking the time to get your nails done!

A horse makes an impressive dance partner...

and is able
to leap tall
fences in a
single bound!

He's a virtual
SUPER HERO!

He will protect you from the bad guys...

and he won't mind if the
good friends hang on.

and make you feel like a queen!

So it might be difficult to find a man that doesn't shy when he hears the word "BRIDLE,"

or one who doesn't bolt at
the thought of being "SADDLED,"

just be sure he'll vow to love and honor you!

Spend your time with a good guy who cherishes all that life has to offer, including you, and enjoy the sunsets together.